Where's Master?

CÆSAR

A Drawing by Maud Earl

From the Photogravure published by the Illustrated London News

Where's Master?

BY

CÆSAR

"I am Cæsar. I belong to the King."

(Inscription on Cæsar's Collar)

HODDER & STOUGHTON
New York & London

To
Master's Queen—and mine ;
To the beautiful Lady who found room
in her poor broken heart
for the sorrow of the
King's little dog
Cæsar.

Where's Master?
I've been hunting for him high and low for days. I can't find Master anywhere, and I'm so lonely. And I'm beginning to hate all these people who pat and pet me and offer me tit-bits to eat. I want Master—he knows just how to rub my hair up the wrong way, just how I like my ears twisted; I want to feel his warm hand catch hold of my

9

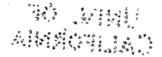

nose and waggle my head slowly
to and fro. I wouldn't let anyone else do that, but he knows
just how to find the little
ticklish place under my chin.
They have just brought me my
dinner. They say She ordered
it specially for me. I must
say it smelt good, and I thought
I'd try a mouthful to please
Her. But it tasted bitter like
medicine.

I want a bone from Master's
plate. I never worry him when
he's at table, but he knows I'm
always there beside the right
leg of his chair. And Master

never forgets his little dog, however many important people he
may have to feed.

I've searched the Palace
from top to bottom. At first it
was rather fun, like the hide-
and-seek game I used to play
when I was a puppy. I pretended I knew all the time
where he was, and that I was
running up the stairs and along
the corridors and into room
after room just for the sport of
it all. But I'm getting too old
for that sort of thing. I've had
a very jolly life, but I've had a
lot to do and think about—

Master has been a bit of a care
you know, and I've worried a
good deal about him lately —
and oh! I feel very tired and
very sad and I want. Master
badly. Where *is* Master?

At first I thought he was still in the bedroom where I left him that Friday afternoon, and then I made sure he was in the Throne room, the great room with the slippery floor where I have to walk very carefully on the tips of my nails. But I must have been mistaken, for though I whined for quite a long time outside each door, and even gave just a short little bark, Master never

13

came. Sometimes he does keep me waiting a little just to tease me, but I've only to give a loud snuffle in the crack between the door and the floor, and the littlest scratch on the panel, and however busy he is he'll let me in. I'm awfully afraid I left my mark on the Throne room door, but I hope it won't be noticed, and, if it is, Master will put it all right, for he'll be very cross when he finds out they wouldn't let his little dog in. I know there was someone inside, for I heard voices just like those I've listened to while Master was in

14

church and I was outside waiting
for him. I've always tried to be
a specially good dog on Sunday,
but Master says I've never
been quite good enough to take
inside church—though I've been
almost everywhere else with
him.

hat a fine time we had at Sandringham only a Sunday or two ago. I thought Master seemed tired at break-fast, and I wanted him so much to take a rest that morning; so I snuggled up very close to him in his chair and pretended to snore. When he said, "This won't do, Cæsar, you know, it's Church time," I took no notice, but put my paws across his knees and my nose on my paws and

16

yawned. "I'm sorry, old man,"
Master said, "I'm tired too. I've
done a bit too much lately, and
there is still so much to be done.
But I must go to Church, you
know."

I didn't take any notice,
and his voice was so low and
weary that I thought if I
kept very still and breathed
very hard, as if I were fast
asleep, he might rest too. For
a minute or two he sat quite
still. Then he jumped up and
sent me flying, and said, quite
sharply for him, "You know I
never miss Church on Sunday."

And I did know, but I wish
I could have kept him indoors
that Sunday morning, for it was
a cold, damp day and, somehow,
I felt low and miserable and I
wanted him to myself. But I
knew, too, that, when he spoke
like that, not even his little dog
could stop him. He is always
very kind, but he's always
Master and no one ever thinks
of disobeying him.

I saw him off at the door. I
suppose I looked pretty down,
for I remember he turned back
and gave my ear a pull and
promised he'd take me for a

real good walk in the afternoon.

And then I went to have a
talk with Daisy, who lives at
Sandringham, and who is a very
decent dog for a smooth-haired
terrier. My hair is wiry and
very rough. The funny thing
is I found Daisy miserable and
worried too. As a matter of
fact she was rather bad-tem-
pered and growled when she
saw me, but I soon settled that,
for I don't stand any nonsense.
She said she had dreamed all
night long, horrid nightmary
dreams about drowned puppies,

that when she woke she thought
she saw the moon crying, and
began to howl. "It was just a
boy with a stable lantern," I
laughed. "It may have been,"
she replied, "but it's the same
dream I dreamt and the same
moon I saw two days before
that day when the poor old
gentleman died as he was
watching the guns." "You're
an old woman," said I, "your
liver is out of order. Go and
chew some grass."

I did have a grand time that Sunday afternoon at San-dringham. Master and I went everywhere about the grounds. He seemed to want to see every-thing, all the new things that had been planted, all the new arrangements that were being planned. He was in such good spirits, too, that I forgot myself and scratched up a big stone in one of the walks right in front of the gardener's nose. I ran

to and fro over the flower beds
too, and pretended to smell a
rat, and dug a great hole in a
newly sown grass plot and
scattered the mould all over
the path.

And Master just laughed
and said, "You're a nice scamp
to upset everything just as I was
having it tidied up for Her to
see." He was in great spirits
that afternoon was Master; he
talked and joked with every-
body, and made the Agent laugh
so once that I fairly danced with
delight. Master's got the most
catchable laugh in the world,

but somehow lately he has
seemed too tired to laugh much.
I nearly went mad with joy
when I heard him, and I caught
hold of Daisy's ear and chased
her round and round till we both
dropped dead beat at his feet.
"It's time to go home," thought
I, "this weather is treacherous.
I've got a touch of rheumatism
in my off hind leg, and it's beginning to tweak. That's a
danger signal."

"Come along, Master," I said,
"it's damp under foot and there's
a horrid mist rising, and I want
to sit and toast in front of the

fire. I want to sit juſt by your feet and ſtare at the flames and see all sorts of exciting things in the fire till my head sways and nods and nods and I almoſt tumble, and then wake up to ſtare at the flames and watch the battles in the coal again."

And so while Maſter was looking at one of the new roads they are cutting I turned towards home and began to walk away in the hope that he'd follow me almoſt without knowing. As he didn't move, I went back and juſt rubbed my nose gently againſt his trousers. I love

those rough things he wears at
Sandringham—they don't show
my hairs as his uniforms and
black suits do.

I know he understood, for
he gave me a little push with
his foot—just fancy if anyone
but Master dared to touch me
with his foot!—and said some-
thing about a lazy young rascal,
but instead of coming home he
turned to the Agent, and said,
"Show me *everything*. I want to
see everything, and arrange
everything for the year, so that
She may find everything ready
when She comes down."

That evening after dinner Master did rest for a few minutes. I was so comfy, curled up just behind his knees on the sofa. And then if some-one didn't bring him a pile of papers, and he worked and worked and worked while I nodded in front of the fire. If only I could have helped him a little. I got up once and put my paws on his knees, and tried to see what he was doing, but he laughed a little sadly as he said, "Affairs of State, Cæsar —rather above the head of a little dog." I gave his hand a tiny lick to show I understood, but as I watched the lines on Master's face I thought to myself, "And very bad for the head of dear Master too." But as I've heard them say so many times lately, "That's what comes of being a King."

I couldn't sleep that night. My bed was all knobs and creases. I trampled it down, round and round, but I couldn't get it really as I like it. I

always sleep in Master's bedroom, and I pity anyone who
dares to disturb him in the
night. It may have been the
supper I had—I always eat too
much when I'm in the country
—or it may have been the talk
I had with Daisy. Anyway,
just as I was getting off to sleep
in the early morning, I started
up, and every hair on my back
stood on end, for in the corner
of the room I saw a strange dark
shadow. I bared my teeth and
growled as fiercely as I could.
"Lie still, Cæsar," said the
voice from the bed, "I've got a
bit of a cough, old man, and

that's what's disturbed you."
But Master didn't see what I
saw, and I stopped awake all
night long ready to spring at
that dark shadow. But it never
moved. It seemed to be waiting
and watching, watching Master
as he tossed uneasily on his bed.
And I waited and watched the
shadow.

I snuggled close inside Master's thick coat next morning in the train. I was beautifully warm, but I could feel he was shivering, while his hand on my head felt hot. And every time I began to doze I was shaken awake by his cough. "Sorry, Cæsar," he'd say, "you'd better go to sleep by yourself on that seat opposite." I pretended I was not a bit tired and snuggled all the closer to see if I couldn't keep Master warm. He seemed so cold. "You'd better see a Vet when you get home," thought I. "I don't like that cough. I had a cough, too, once, and I felt as if I had been beaten all over. I remember the Vet said they must keep me in what he called an even temperature. I don't know what that is, but for me, at any rate, it meant lots of cosetting, a gorgeous fire, a special blanket tucked round me, and the daintiest food—such a time in fact that I kept up that cough for weeks and even now when I'm not satisfied with my meals I can bring it on again if I try very hard."

I believe Master wanted an even temperature, but instead of that as soon as we got to London, I saw him changing to go out again somewhere into the wet and cold. I suppose he had to. It was one of those terrible things he calls "a long standing engagement." I'm glad I have no long-standing engagements, and can curl myself up and go to sleep just when I want to. I'm glad I am only the King's little dog. Oh! I'm so glad I'm not a King.

here *is* Master. He must have gone for a long journey all alone by himself, for I've been all over the Palace and everyone else seems here. But then that's impossible, for he never went anywhere without his little dog. I remember some of my friends have told me how miserable they are when they see boxes and portmanteaux. It means they are to be left behind in the care of someone who half starves them, and only takes them out for ten minutes a day on a string. But I just yelp for pure joy

when I see signs of packing up,
for that means a trip with
Master to Brighton, Paris,
Biarritz, Marienbad, I don't
care where. All that I care
about is that it means a rest for
Master and more of Master,
so much more, for his little dog.

They are bringing boxes into
the Palace, and there is bustle
and movement everywhere.
But I can't make it out. I smelt
one of the packages, and there
were flowers inside. It was a
sickly, dead smell.

By the way, I haven't smelt

Master's cigar for days. How's
that, I wonder? The last time
I smelt that cigar—you can trust
Master's little dog to know that
scent among a million—was on
that Friday afternoon when the
man in the long black coat
wanted to keep me out of
Master's room.

I tried to push past him
through the door, but he told
someone to hold me back. I
snarled.

"That's the King's physician,"
I heard them say. "And I'm
the King's dog," I said, and I

barked and snapped at the people at the door. I knew Master wanted me.

"Let Cæsar come in at once," I heard him say, and they stood back and let me through. I made one of them skip as I passed, I can tell you. I was in a bit of a temper for I'm not used to being kept waiting.

Master was sitting up in a chair. There were three or four black-coated men around him, and the room smelt so funny. She was there, standing beside the chair. I saw he had his

36

boots on, and I thought at first
he was waiting for me to go for
a walk with him, for he hadn't
been outside the Palace since
the day we came back from
Sandringham. I jumped round
the room and barked for joy.
"Hush, little man," said She,
"Master's not at all well."

"I'm all right," I heard his
voice reply, only it seemed to me
so hollow and far away. "Let
him be. Here, Cæsar. Do you
want to go out, out, out?" Didn't
I just? But I looked at Her, at
them all, and I saw they wanted
to keep Master quiet and get

him to rest, so I yawned and
flopped down beside his chair
as if I were too stiff to stir.

He had a dreadful fit of
coughing, and then when it was
over he bent over and patted my
head and said, " I'm a bit tired
to-day myself, old man. I suppose we'll have to do as we're
told, you and I, and keep quiet
and warm indoors. But it's no
good talking. I've a long-standing engagement for this evening
that I must keep. . . . . Well,
well, give me a cigar, I'll
promise to rest for a bit. No,
no, Cæsar can stay, of course."

I watched at Master's feet
for—well, it seemed hours,
but I almost held my breath for
fear of disturbing him, and it
may have been only minutes.
And then some one carried me
out and called me a poor little
dog. I was too sleepy to mind.
And I haven't seen Master
since.

aster's dead. Oh, yes, I know what that means. I know so well that I wish, I wish so much, that I could die too. Some stupid person came and told me a long story about Master having gone away, but I just yawned in his face. Master *doesn't* go away without his little dog. If he did, I'd follow him, and I'd find him. I know he's still here in the Palace, although they won't let me see him, and yet I feel it's not Master who is here, it's only a little part of *my* Master who is here.

Master, my real Master, has gone somewhere where I can't follow. There's a great big river between Master and me, a river I can't swim; a great big wall, a wall I can't climb. I think he must want me a little bit, and oh! I want him so badly. Where *is* Master?

She has told me. Master's dead. I shall never see him or feel him again. And She is sorrowing for Master too, just the same, only more—so much more because she is a Human, and Humans have bigger hearts to break than poor little dogs. I've only a tiny heart, but it was full of love for dear Master. And dear Master is dead. I've no Master now. I've nothing, no one, to live for. Master is dead.

I'm so miserable. I can't rest. I've just been wandering about the stables. On the way I met one of those foreign dogs they keep there. Thought I to myself, a fight, especially a fight with a foreigner, just fits in with my temper — I've been a tremendous fighter in my time. So I began to dance towards the creature very slowly, on the tips of my toes, with my legs and my tail very straight and stiff, and my hair on end, and drawing my breath in very loudly. It's the correct thing in a square fight to give the

enemy time to get ready. And
then somehow, I couldn't go on.
For I remembered Master and
the way he talked to me at
Biarritz when I started to tackle
a French poodle, an over-
dressed thing all tied up with
ribbons.

"What a typical Englishman
you are, Cæsar," said Master,
"you can't meet a foreigner
without beginning to growl, and
strut about as if the whole world
had been created just for you.
Now, look here, I'm tired of all
this snarling and fighting, and
you've just got to make friends

instead of going about everywhere quarrelling with every
dog whose looks you don't
approve of."

And Master actually made
me walk quietly beside him
along the Plage, while he called
to the Frenchman to come and
walk with him on the other
side. Then after I'd got used
to the chap he left us alone
together, and really he wasn't at
all a bad kind of a dog and he
certainly knew how to make
himself very pleasant. To my
surprise, too, I discovered he
was very sensible in spite of his

airs. He actually knew quite a lot of things I didn't, though of course I didn't give myself away, and I got one or two useful tips from him. I was really sorry to say good-bye to him in the end.

And Master did just the same with that Russian he keeps at Sandringham, and with those long sausage-shaped things with short legs they call hounds in Germany. Of course I could fight and beat the whole lot of them if I tried, but I'm beginning to see it's rather a silly game to make enemies when you can just as easily make friends.

And so when I came up to the foreigner in the stable yard I wagged my tail, and we rubbed noses and went in together to see Master's charger, Kildare. I found the foreign chap was nearly as sorry about Master as I was. It wasn't the same sorrow, you know, but it was very real.

They were dressing up
Kildare in her best, and
giving her an extra-special rub
down. Master's starting on his
last journey to-day, they say,
and Kildare goes with him.

If only I might go with him
too. Little dogs never march in
a procession, they tell me. But
then, no little dog ever loved his
Master as I do, and no Master
was like my Master.

She says I can go if I am very good and follow close behind Master, and walk very slowly, and never move from the middle of the road. Oh, how glad and thankful I am. I wonder if Master knows, and is pleased that, after all, his little dog is going with him on his last journey.

I'm so frightened. I've never been afraid before in my life. I've seen crowds before, huge crowds, but never a crowd like this. They always used to shout and wave their hats. But these people are silent as,—why, silent as Death.

I recognise lots of people who are waiting outside the Church. There's the King who went shooting with Master lately, and there's the other King who talked so solemnly with him over in Germany. And there's the man they call the, Prime Minister. He doesn't know me, but I shan't forget in a hurry the day he came to Brighton. When he left I watched him from the window, walking on the front. It was then that Master said to me, "If you could talk, Cæsar, you could tell some surprising things, couldn't you?" I should think I could, but Master knew I wouldn't if I could. He always trusted me with all his secrets.

No one takes any notice of Master's little dog. I'm so lonely beside this man in kilts. Kilts make me think of the moors, and the times we had together in Scotland. Master looked so splendid in kilts, and he was always so happy when he wore them.

I think I shall just put my tail tight between my legs and try and creep away somewhere, away from all these people and these uniforms.

Now good and kind She is. She has just been and patted me, and told me to be a brave dog, and hold myself up straight, for I'm the King's dog.

Do you know, I had almost forgotten. I belong to the King. I mustn't let Master, my King, be ashamed of his little dog to-day. How beautifully Kildare is marching. He's so proud to be here. And I'm proud too but oh, so very, very sad, for this is my last journey with Master.

I'm marching in front of the Kings. I've no history, I've no pedigree, I'm not high-born. But I loved him, and I was faithful to him, and he didn't care how lowly or humble man or beast might be as long as they did their best and were faithful.

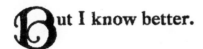e've come to the end of the journey. They say I can't follow Master any further. They say there are no little dogs where Master has gone.

But I know better.

Printed at The Edinburgh Press, 68 Old Bailey, London, E C.

Milton Keynes UK
Ingram Content Group UK Ltd.
UKHW012136080224
437403UK00005B/50